At My Heart, A Turquoise Lake

By Catherine Veritas

To Kara Masters, smiling inspiration
To Marshall Bliss, Teacher and friend
To my patients

In the silence of the night comes the Unknown She, whispering sweetly, "*Come dance with me.*" Lynn Barron

Contents

At My Heart, A Turquoise Lake

Turquoise Woman

Turquoise woman
pipe-stone woman
blood of earth woman
fire woman
I am fortress
to those who challenge
sublime beauty
to those who see
I garner blessings from true power
sacred will my journey be

Invocation

I turn my face to the rising sun
I am full mind and full body
toward south I bow
knowing that many have walked
this spirit path before me
they smile upon me now
my gaze turns inward
Thunder Beings move
I am the eye of the storm
my word is gentle
and unstoppable
as oncoming winter

Kilauea Crater

Monday I walked the sacred ground of
Pu'uhonua o Honaunau
Place of Refuge
where any who broke kapu
could be cleansed of transgression
there I bid good peace to the past
Tuesday I visited Kilauea Crater
Home of Pelehonuamea
Goddess of Fire
Pele of the Sacred Land
I stood at the lip of Her crater
with prayerful yearning and
plumeria offerings
admiring Her magnificent white veil
soaring plume of sulfuric steam
I edged past cruise-line buses
Japanese tour groups
the lot of parked cars
seeking an unobstructed view

"see my heart" I beseeched Pelehonuamea
"I am a pipe-carrier" I offered
as a badge of my worthiness
and there I stood
in windy
swirling
silence
until I remembered
I Am the Pipe
expanding my awareness
solar plexus
womb
hips
earth
I became the sacred bowl
of blood and fire
my core straightening like a rod
the pipe stem
toward heaven
in an inkling
what was unseen became seen

within a flickering, chuckling flow
a rumbling, red-orange glow
I heard "Oh, little caldera."

long moments I bathed in
awesome presence
trembling joy and gratitude
to be acknowledged
Fire Queen to little fire

two days later
Alika, guardian of the Western Gate
(also security guard at Kona airport)
questioned me
had I felt the sacred energy of Hawaii?
how had I prepared myself?
he listened carefully then we embraced
Alika saying, you are beautiful
come back to us

now I greet mighty Pelehonuamea
whenever I mark the seven directions

I bow to Her in the West
where I honor the ThunderBeings
of the Plains
and the EarthShakers of the San Andreas

I will always remember Pelehonuamea's
great generosity

in greeting me

a visitor to Her land
at that time
as my own creative fire boiled and
yearned
to flow out into the world
a fountain of beauty and light

Solar Eclipse

At the edge of the eclipse
Jaguar beckons
I ponder warrior women before me
knowing that I, too, have been called
to the task
Jaguar flings heavy doors wide
and we step through
to enter the Sun
facing each other
eye to eye
we become
stillness
in the midst of the solar fire
even Gaia Herself
is nourished
in the moment of repose

Riverstone

I flash in sunlight
I sing in fire
I laugh at my tarnish
I splash through desires
I'm a stone
tumbling down this river of life
with a center as sure
as the point of a knife
I'm tumbling down this river
sometimes with glee
because I'm grinding off periphery
till all that's left is me

Vision

His flesh writhes with raw memory
yet the man stands
silent and still
a tree among trees
I weep, and I kneel
the dark cat beckons
we are off at a run
to a place of his choosing
"This is your teaching"
midnight cat speaks
before becoming
himself
still as white stone
unseen hands press my skin into quartz
my limbs into rock
my mind into stone
my cells re-tuned
to a crystalline structure
we return to the trees
Jaguar and I
moving with graceful, sleek stealth

I am drawn to the intensity
of unhealed wounds
dark fur steadies me
I sink roots into earth
becoming
myself
a tree among trees
silent and still
"This is your teaching," Jaguar speaks
in gratitude I offer the sacred tobacco
and the night dark cat leaps into my heart

Anger

Your flip response
brief clench of the jaw
or
silence
that means all my unspoken fears
my fury
on self-inflating auto-pilot
expands instantaneously
I stand
hip-fisted
disdainfully-flaming eyes
appalled that we are here
yet again
if
you could remain calm
risk
a skillfully gentle joke
I might

just
might
find a way
to step back
let go
begin again

Grief's Wanting

I was strangling myself
with my own emotion
I didn't know
inside the dark intensity of my grief
I had no clue
it was my hand upon the tether
pulling tighter and tighter
imagine my dismay
my awe
when in the midst of emotional
asphyxiation
some recess of my mind
threw me a lifeline
as my hand loosed the noose
to take hold the line
(of poetry)
steely fingers
revealed empty palms
and I witnessed grief's soft underbelly
the velvet, vulnerable belly-fur of a
trusting cat

yearning
for love

Here the words of my poetic salvation
Remember
You are the one
you have been waiting for
who can love all you have ever been
all you are now
and all you will ever be

Night of the Dark Eclipse

I beseech the guardian
Spirit of Jaguar
do not let me enter that night black room
from which there is no escape
without the eyes to see
beyond appearances
into the Light
into the heart of the matter
for though I cannot see to find my step
I must continue on
breathing and loving
for that
(they say)
is everything

A Rainy Weekend Reading Dee Brown's "Bury My Heart At Wounded Knee"

Chief Little Crow was murdered
for bounty
his head garishly displayed
in downtown St. Paul
land of my forefathers

my heart breaks to know this

with stinging eyes I recall
what Oscar Wilde said
Hearts are made to be broken

outside my window
the rain slows to a stop
hummingbird swoops
at encroaching flycatchers
her precious clutch bounces precarious
on the whipping wind

as a young boy, Sitting Bull vowed
to protect the buffalo country
already knowing the end of that story
my heart
breaks
more

the cherub face of a missing child
flashes across my screen
New Details Have Emerged
I don't want to know
I click off the computer
return to reading

the mother and father of Crazy Horse
buried his heart
along a creek called Wounded Knee
where 13 years later
the 7th Cavalry Regiment slaughtered
Big Foot's tattered band
of Ghost Dancers
in the snow

four days after Christmas

how can our hearts not be broken

my niece calls
weeping for a man
who promised perfect love
but left her nothing

Hearts are made to be broken

sometimes I cling to
what Oscar Wilde said
lest I seek a place
to bury my own

(To paraphrase Oscar Wilde: *The tragedy is not that hearts break; the tragedy is when hearts turn into stone.*)

Venus Transits the Sun 2012

(next Venus Transit 2117)

Spirit woman speaks to me
sometimes it's hard for a young person
so full of life and expectation
to die
anxiously I grip her hand
my body feels stuffed with ghosts
memories
worries
fears
distend before me like a bloated gut

the instant the orb of Venus
penetrates the sphere of flame
my burden begins to dissemble
separating into parts
crumbling to dust
dissolving into mud

Spirit woman gathers the remnants of my
precious years
offering them up to the summer sun

She cracks open my skull
picking through bones
ensuring that all is sacrificed
to the solar fire
She keeps vigil now
as angels descend the portal of Venus'
shadow
to perform sacred surgery
afterward Spirit woman binds my wounds
and assists me to stand
my center
has been repositioned
higher

Spirit woman speaks to me
lift your heart above discord
you will grow strong with the effort
and wherever you go
sow seeds
sow seeds of beauty
and light

Ignorance

I cannot save you from yourself
is an odd thought
when Self
is
the center of the wheel
and the doorway through
why keep you from your own personal
swan-dive
or wish caution in your pursuit of oblivion
why not shout
run quickly toward the fire of annihilation

I surrender my preference
my ignorance

Recipe for Flying Ointment

Skin of bufo
snatch of Tuvo
drunken-toungue blabber
want, flaunted and bare
do I dodge or banter
my blithe boundary-crasher
sweet
like sticky-candy fingers
on a melt-blacktop day

My Dream Last Night

What was it you told me
in my dream last night
that made me smile through my pores
remembering goodness instead of loss
I can't recall the words
but they are inside me
bleaching long-set blood stains
of un-meant harm
of tangled misunderstanding
of our untimely love

At My Heart, A Turquoise Lake

At my heart
rests a turquoise lake
an eye of stillness greets me
peace permeates the web
of all my relations
bliss is remembered
truth and laughter entwined
adorned in beauty
I dance
weaving light into my dreams
offering them into the web of all things

Gaia Said

Gaia said
it is me you feel
when you stand upon
Kilauea's sacred ground
it is me you feel
when your knees buckle
before the ancient temple Hagar Qim
it is me you feel
when you weep for a sunset
or tremble
gazing upon the mountain
standing in regal glory
since before the dawn of time
this life
these feelings
these experiences
I give to you
let me be your motive
for I am your bliss

On the Completion of My Novel

No congratulatory banner
no rousing embrace
Spirit woman seats me opposite
across the open fire ring
look, she says, pointing
the egg of fire and light we have been
tending
the fruit of my long labor
has broken open
its precious contents
gone
sudden exhaustion pools my every bone
a sob sighs through my belly
now empty and raw
as if my own womb has birthed
the creature light
which has flown from this place
Spirit woman stands
stepping into the still-warm fire ring
it's alright, she says to my dismay
I am a fire-woman

she extends her hand to me, saying
as are you
I join her inside the ring
amidst pieces of shell
and smoldering embers
flames ignite
engulfing our bodies
we are fire-women, she whispers
staving my fear
as the fire burns through

burning me clean
burning me clean

The Way

Love me
speaks the Christ
more than you love
your unhealed wounds
isn't that the message of salvation
that my Way show-er bears the form
of fair-haired Jesus
ancient dark-skinned saint
or white light of High Self
matters not one jot
love is love
light is light

love me
speaks the Christ
heart unveiled
brightness blinding
more than you love
unhealed wounds

inside That brilliance
I see
the truth
where I am caught
and the pathway through

Imperfect

We are imperfect
you and I
sure we love crystalline order
yes we dig the structure of time
we simply flow beyond those boundaries
we create Art
translating beautiful truths
in a free and feminine dance
of daring
and discipline
undulating change
and heart-felt spirit-offerings
listen, sister
be without anxiety about imperfection
love all you see—feel—imagine
trust your intentions
forgive the chaos of becoming
and allow yourself to be amazed
by the beauty of creation

Languid

Languid
is my new mantra
I'm applying it everywhere
      languid thinking
      languid worry
      languid breath
when I looked up the word I found
the synonyms
to be : weak, anemic, and slack
that's not what I mean!
      I mean sensual, slow
      and non-attached
      the opposite of desperate, anxious
      and tense
I'm sticking to my version of the word for
now

I'll practice my
     languid thinking
     languid worry (try it yourself)
     languid breath
and thus make my inner world
a more generous
and hospitable
dwelling place

I Gave Up Thinking For Lent

I gave up *thinking* for Lent
if Carol can give up chocolate
and Joyce can give up on-line shopping
I can give up *thinking*
given my strong-willed mind
and its life-long habit
I decided to fine myself for *thinking*
a quarter
a dime
any loose change would make the point
hearing a nickel clank
into the Tibetan bowl
really gets my attention
now noticing a thought is not the same
thing as *thinking*
as I'm meaning it
thinking is grabbing hold of a thought
chewing on it
repeating it with subtle nuance
pinning it to a bulletin board
like a moth display
of course, some of my thoughts are

so damn satisfying
I'll pay a quarter
and stay for the whole show
but often my brand of *thinking*
is a tedious, anxiety-provoking affair
best to drop in a dime
and leave right away
sometimes if a thought is emotionally
charged
I have to use real muscle to work with it
like this morning
and my pissed-off-ness at an unexpected
change in plans
after the usual tactics failed
I mentally yelled, "Don't Think!
Don't Think!"
the words discharging like smoke-bombs
under the cover of smoke and noise
I managed to connect with my breath
breathing while pissed is fine
repeatedly reworking my grievance
is what I'm trying to avoid

look at all the things I can do without
thinking
I can play the piano or listen to music
groom my shedding cat
or sit and watch the beauty of the day
I can exercise
or draw
I can even write a poem
like this one
as long as I put down what comes easily
I didn't say I couldn't concentrate
in fact, not-*thinking*, for me
involves quite a lot of concentration
left to itself
my (brilliant, wayward) mind
loves to think
excels at thinking
wants to *solve* all manner of things by
thinking
I'm trying something different now
something more soothing to the soul

at this age I'd like to take
all my breaths more fully
smile more easily
and shed the burdensome illusion
that my every thought and decision
are of monumental importance
to my fate and the fate of the world

Last Quarter

The moon wanes before it grows
the tide ebbs before it flows
this is the time of letting go
this is the time to free your mind
release the push
your will, unbind
that which is already in motion
will spiral through
and soon you will begin anew
but now you must yield
to the surrendered flow
this is the time of letting go

Crone Song

Through gnarled root
crone whispers
come to me
know your depth
love the earth
come to me
in flash of fire
crone howls
come to me
love your heat
own your crown
come to me
she chants
come as you are
despite fear or regret
bring your fierce hard-earned *No*
your exultant wild *Yes*
cross the threshold and bid
good peace to the past
the crone song calls
come to me

Heartwings

No angel wings of brilliant white
no fairy wings of gossamer light
my wings, dusky brown, are sturdy and
strong
determined and mighty, not in size but in
brawn
they can lurch into headwind
they can fly through a storm
even beat-down and bedraggled
my wings still perform
when I'm swept into rapids of emotional
pain
I call my heartwings for unerring
elevation gain
my heart has wings of pelican-brown
they've been tested and tried
and will not let me down
they allow me my dramas
my griefs, my strife
yet ever when called
help me choose love
help me choose life

Blessing

Love life
more than you
grieve suffering

celebrate power inside you
more than you
reject its corruption in others

let your pleasure
in sex
transform all history of its abuse

may the experience of bliss
nourish you
and sustain you
all the days of your life

Los Angeles Goodbye

Thank you for the opportunity
to be born among your concrete towers
lullabied by your freeways' roar
for against the backdrop
of made-by-man
examining the soft, supple
infinitely
ever-evolving Self
became a worthy
and compelling challenge
facing gridlocked traffic
and the grid of societal expectation
I moved to secret inner rhythms
finding a winding way
to the center of my being
laugh with me
as I bask in
the Now
here
myself, a beautiful cog
in your kaleidoscope of Angels

and kiss me gently
as I step off your turning wheel
bidding Adios
and thanks
to you
my Ciudad de La Reina de Los Angeles
my City of the Queen of The Angels

Prayer

Thank you for this day
on the garden planet
thank you for life
for love in all its flavors
for the worthy challenge of being human
help me remember my union
with that which gives rise to this world
my union with fire
and rock
and Gaia's sacred heart within
spread forgiveness
for the errors of humanity
as we seek our way
through all that surrounds us
and continue to heal us
thrill us
amaze us
with the beauty of creation

Catherine Veritas is the author of *The Maltese Dreamer*, a mystical-historical fiction, and a painter of transformational art. For 32 years she practiced the healing arts of Holistic Chiropractic in Los Angeles, California. She now practices art and healing on the Big Island of Hawaii.

www.CatherineVeritas.com
Facebook:
Catherine Veritas – art of healing.

Thank you Maata Lynne Barron, Sufi teacher, for the opening quote.